CANADIAN FOLK ART

OLD WAYS IN A NEW LAND

D1261693

CANADIAN FOLK ART

OLD WAYS IN A NEW LAND

Michael Bird

Toronto
OXFORD UNIVERSITY PRESS
1983

Canadian Cataloguing in Publication Data
Bird, Michael S., 1941–
    Canadian folk art

Bibliography: p.
ISBN 0-19-540424-6

1. Folk art – Canada.   I. Title.

NK841.B57   745'.0971   C83-098537-9

All photographs are by the author, except for the following:

British Columbia Provincial Museum: p. 30.
Guy Couture: p. 70.
Henry and Barbara Dobson: pp. 19, 62, 67, 113.
Glenbow Museum: p. 60.
Hobb's Photography: pp. 75, 103.
Montreal Museum of Fine Arts: pp. 96-7.
National Gallery of Canada: pp. 8, 10, 54.
The Redemptorist Fathers: pp. 90-1, 92-3.
Royal Ontario Museum: pp. 20-1, 39, 108.

© Oxford University Press Canada 1983
1 2 3 4 - 6 5 4 3
Designed by Heather Delfino
Printed in Hong Kong by
EVERBEST PRINTING COMPANY LIMITED

CONTENTS

ACKNOWLEDGEMENTS

This book would not have been possible without the assistance of a great many people, and I regret that restrictions of space prohibit me from mentioning everyone by name. Above all, I am indebted to Terry Kobayashi, for her artistic judgement and innate sense of what constitutes 'good' folk art. I would also like to express special gratitude to J. Russell Harper, Dr Louis C. Jones, Nancy-Lou Patterson, Nettie Sharpe, and Pastor Frederick S. Weiser.

Most of the objects in this book are in private collections. For their generosity in supplying artifacts, information, or both, I am grateful to Peter and Maggie Bell, Clay and Carol Benson, Fred and Dora Mae Blayney, Louis Bolduc, William and Caroline Byfield, Mona Carroll, Ron and Wendy Cascaden, Carole Clarke, Jowe and Pauline Creighton, John and Vikki Forbes, Hyla and Walter Fox, John and Anne Hall, John and Heather Harbinson, Jim and Norma Hiscock, Charles and Gay Humber, Emile Lessard, Marjorie and Clarence Larmon, Norman and Barbara Macdonald, Lloyd Ryder, Wolfgang and Carroll Schlombs, Nettie Sharpe, and Robert and Brenda Star, as well as those who asked to remain anonymous. Many individuals associated with museums, galleries, archives, and historical societies also rendered invaluable assistance. Among them are Jean-François Blanchette, Paul Carpentier, Pierre Crépeau, Magnus Einarsson, Richard Field, Conrad Graham, Joan Mattie, Wesley Mattie, Scott Robson, Barbara Schneider, Gary Selig, Philip Tilney, and William Yeager. Finally, I would like to thank my editors at Oxford University Press, Richard Teleky and Sally Livingston.

MICHAEL BIRD

INTRODUCTION

'You can take all the pictures you like if you'll just do some dusting—and maybe a little vacuuming too. I'm afraid I haven't done the spring cleaning yet.' The owner shook her head in disbelief when she saw the fine piece of *Fraktur* I wanted to photograph: 'Will *that* really go into a book?' Over years of studying folk art, I have often heard people express real surprise that a world of museums and art galleries could ever be interested in their old hand-me-downs. But that is only one of the many apparent contradictions associated with folk art.

In a sense, the term 'folk art' itself is paradoxical. The first word suggests something common and ordinary, belonging to the people, while the second implies the unique quality of individual inspiration. This fundamental division is reflected in the contradictory characteristics that any definition of this 'uncommon art of common people'[1] must include.

A mixture of naïvety and sophistication, tradition and innovation, cultural repetition and individual invention, folk art has a way of looking simultaneously backwards to the past and ahead to new applications. In fact, sustained tension between these elements seems to be a feature of all the best folk art: works that are purely imitative can be almost as boring as assembly-line products, while those that are radically innovative lose all sense of being rooted in a particular people, culture, or tradition, and become virtually indistinguishable from modern art in general. Nevertheless, within this broad definition any given folk artifact usually shows a leaning in one direction or the other. To express these two basic tendencies we might use the terms 'idiosyncratic'

(individually-centred) and 'ethnosyncratic' (ethnically-centred).

Idiosyncratic folk art is a form of personal expression, and much of its appeal lies in its uniqueness, if not eccentricity. For the collector the focal point is the individual maker, about whom it is often possible, and always desirable, to have some biographical information. The artist may have drawn on any number of sources, from medieval emblems or high-art conventions to illustrated books or even photographs, but what we value is his or her particular vision, imagination, and inventiveness. Broadly speaking, these idiosyncratic qualities are most appreciated in North America, with its long-standing regard for individuality. They are also most evident in contemporary folk art, though by no means confined to it.

Ethnosyncratic folk art, on the other hand, has a collective orientation. Based on the traditional crafts and decorative arts of Europe, it is prized not for its uniqueness but for its similarity to other expressions within a common culture. The value of this kind of folk art does not depend on the artist's personality: however widely two Pennsylvania-German *Fraktur* calligraphers may have differed in period, age, and subjective outlook, their work will differ significantly only in matters of technical competence and modification of detail. Even if one piece is markedly 'better' than another, that difference is less important than the fact that the two share a recognizable cultural context. They are folk art because they are the expression of one particular *folk*. The boundaries of the group—regional, linguistic, or religious—provide the cultural framework within which we identify a given object as a folk artifact: a 'Polish' storage chest, for example, or a 'Mennonite' show towel. We admire works such as these precisely because they so closely resemble others of their type. Their virtue is not a creative departure from the past, but a conservative resistance to change.

Popular discussions of folk art often stress the idea of the 'naïve' or primitive. No doubt part of the reason is that the first exhibitions of folk art in North America took place in the early 1930s, when the art world was still feeling the impact of movements such as cubism and fauvism. It was a period in which the work of Paul Klee, the early Picasso, and the self-taught painter Henri Rousseau had inspired a passion for the naïve and unsophisticated, which many have seen as a protest against the abstraction and intellectualism of high art. Perhaps more thought could be given to the effect of this new sensibility on the interpretation of folk art. Even today, some of the greatest enthusiasts seem to prefer pieces that look as if they might have been made by virtually anyone, almost going out of their way to find signs of limited competence. This kind of folk art has been succinctly described by Kenneth Ames as 'child art on an adult level'.[2]

But if the idea of naïvety, with its emphasis on faulty perspective, tentative execution, and subordination of design to detail, has any bearing on folk art, surely it is more relevant to the individually-centred variety. Consciously or not, we tend to view the latter in relation to high art or popular graphic sources. The reference point of ethnosyncratic folk art, by contrast, lies in traditional crafts. The re-

mark that a piece is 'too good to be folk art' is more likely to be prompted by idosyncratic work than it is by artifacts such as the *Fraktur* bookplate on page 18 or the Doukhobor carpet on page 60. Many ethnically-centred pieces are far from primitive in execution, and may in fact be highly refined.

Closely related to the question of naïvety and refinement is the commonplace dictum that folk art is the product of amateurs. Allowing for the instances in which this is obviously the case, we should remember that a good deal of North American folk art was actually produced by professional craftsmen. Curiously, folk artists of this kind may well have been more common here than in England, for example, where the small geographic area and predominantly urban nature of the civilization left little room for 'provincial' culture. Commenting on the relative rarity of folk art in England, at least one writer[3] has suggested that what there is can be attributed to two distinct groups: unsophisticated craftsmen and aristocratic dabblers. In North America the professional, whether a schoolteacher-calligrapher in Ontario or an itinerant limner in New Brunswick, fell into neither of these categories. His work may have been non-academic, but he did it with moderate to considerable skill.

In any event, the artist's competence is usually a secondary factor in our appreciation of any particular folk artifact: what really attracts us is its power of expression, individual or collective. Personal preferences may differ — the nostalgically-inclined might be drawn to ethnosyncratic folk art, while advocates of the avant-garde often favour the idiosyncratic variety—but the two are equally valid, and both must be included in any general discussion of folk art.

Nevertheless, most of the artifacts in this book are essentially ethnosyncratic. In part this is a result of the decision to leave contemporary folk art largely aside, as a subject deserving serious study in its own right. At the same time, though, the choice of objects seems an accurate reflection of Canada's history as a multicultural nation—one in which different ethnic backgrounds are valued as a source of enrichment for all. From the Maritimes to British Columbia, the range of cultural inspiration is as varied as the mode of expression.

In French Canada, where historically the influence of the church was felt in practically every aspect of life, religious folk art holds a special place. The arts-and-crafts school founded by Bishop Laval at Saint-Joachim (about fifty kilometres south of Montreal) in 1668 was the first anywhere in New France. Although later centuries have produced skilled craftsmen in every field, the art of wood-carving was developed to an outstanding level of proficiency, encompassing every form from wayside crucifixes (pp. 96 and 97) and funeral-carriage decorations (pp. 32-3) to home-made toys (p. 50).

Elsewhere in Canada the folk arts attest to the vitality of other cultural communities. A notable example is that of the Germanic people who founded settlements in Nova Scotia, Ontario, and the prairie provinces. Distinctive styles in architecture, furniture, textiles, and calligraphy, wood-carving, and metal-work indicate the strength of this decorative tradition. Two of the most characteristic forms are the *Fraktur* illumination and the embroidered show towel, both of which typically feature geometric patterns and stylized motifs such as hearts, birds, and flowers in symmetrical arrangements.

The migration of various eastern European groups to the west around the turn of this century gave rise to some of the most intense concentrations of ethnosyncratic folk art in Canada. No doubt the terrible vastness of the prairies reinforced the natural tendency of a transplanted people to look inward and back to the past. Ethnic groups such as the Poles and Ukrainians maintained a rich diversity of decorative traditions, while religious subgroups such as the Mennonites and Doukhobors, despite the external austerity of their lives, managed to foster an inner sense of beauty that found expression in meticulous needlework and calligraphy.

Settlers of English, Scots, and Irish backgrounds—including a good number of United Empire Loyalists—brought a strong British element to Canada's folk art. Faced with the challenge of adapting to new circumstances, these groups responded with a creative mixture of tradition and innovation. Without circumstantial information, it would be hard to tell whether the sampler on page 55 was made in the new world or the old, while the gravemarkers on pages 84-6 are virtually identical to stones carved in New England a century earlier. Captain Alexander McNeilledge's Confederation box (p. 116) on the other hand, is at once clearly Canadian and unmistakably idiosyncratic.

A fascinating by-product of Canada's varied ethnic traditions was the effect they had on the work of native craftsmen. While a representative sampling is beyond the scope of this book, a handful of pieces reflecting a European influence has been included: for example, the quillwork cradle on page 75, in which a Micmac craftswoman incorporated folk-art motifs drawn from the Germanic community of Lunenburg County. The same kind of synthesis of traditional techniques and new subjects can be seen in the Iroquois cradle-board on page 105 and the Haida carving on page 30.

For all its simplicity, folk art appears to offer both the maker and the observer something more than aesthetic enjoyment; it can also provide a sense of order, structure, and continuity. There is little doubt that individuals often experience a kind of self-affirmation through creative activities. At the same time, communities are strengthened by the commonality of their visual arts. As Joan I. Mattie has said of Canadian folk art, 'It seems evident that a people have a need to assure themselves that they have some degree of control over their environment. The very act of incorporating images of environment into subject matter accomplishes this to some degree.'[4] Whether by intent or by fortunate accident, that kind of assurance seems to be a perennial feature of folk art.

The cliché that Canada is a land of many faces is true in more ways than one. In fact, the face revealed through this country's folk art could hardly be more different from the one presented in much of our literature. We are all familiar with the image of Canada as a bush garden, a desolate landscape, a hostile wilderness; novelists and poets have portrayed Canadians, pioneer and contemporary alike, as a people preoccupied with survival. Could such a people really have produced the self-affirming art displayed in the following pages? On the contrary, the work of Canada's folk artists suggests that their energies were far from exhausted by the effort required for subsistence. The artifacts in this book confirm that Canada was not built by the woodsman's axe and the homesteader's plough alone; at the same time it was created by the knife and chisel, the pen and brush, the needle and scissors — the simple tools with which ordinary people gave their everyday life a modest beauty.

NOTES

[1] Beatrix T. Rumford, 'Uncommon Art of the Common People: A Review of Trends in the Collecting and Exhibiting of American Folk Art', in Ian M.G. Quimby and Scott T. Swank, eds., *Perspectives on American Folk Art* (New York: W.W. Norton & Co., 1980), 226.

[2] Kenneth Ames, *Beyond Necessity: Art in the Folk Tradition* (Winterthur, Del.: The Winterthur Museum, 1977), 96.

[3] James Ayres, *British Folk Art* (Woodstock, N.Y.: The Overlook Press, 1977), 11.

[4] Joan I. Mattie, *Folk Art in Canada* (Plattsburgh, N.Y.: The Clinton County Historical Museum, 1981), 3.

1

PAINTINGS, DRAWINGS, & PAPER CUT-OUTS

Before cameras and commercial reproductions were widely available,
anyone wanting a portrait of a loved one,
a memento of the family home,
or simply a picture to brighten the wall
usually had to rely on the efforts
of self-taught amateur or semi-professional artists.
The painted portraits and landscapes,
miscellaneous drawings,
and ornate paper cut-outs in this section
represent a broad range of work,
from naïve interpretations of academic art
to imaginative expressions of individual personalities.

PORTRAIT OF ALFRED BARKER
Thomas MacDonald
c. 1830
New Brunswick
18.5 × 13 cm

A travelling artist, Thomas MacDonald painted a number of
watercolour portraits in the Fredericton-Gagetown area. Rarely is
the influence of high art on folk art as clear as it is in a work like
this, with its formal pose and drapery background. The use of
props—in this case a music book—to indicate the sitter's status
or vocation is another classical convention.

PORTRAIT OF ANN S. SMITH
Thomas MacDonald
c. 1830
New Brunswick
17.5 × 13 cm

This watercolour portrait shows the artist's sensitivity to the youth of his subject; the open outdoor setting and simple floral detail suggest a child's world. One of the few itinerant limners in Canada, MacDonald ranks with the finest New England practitioners of the craft.

WALL PAINTING
Anonymous
c. 1848
Granville Ferry, Nova Scotia
210 × 380 × 450 cm
Courtesy National Gallery of Canada

Probably derived from European overmantel paintings and landscape wallpapers of the eighteenth century, oil-on-plaster murals were popularized in New England by artists such as Rufus Porter (1792–1884). Examples are rare in Canada, but a few have been found in the Annapolis Valley area. This wall from the William Croscup house includes two family scenes: the Croscup marriage, attended by a piper, and Mrs Croscup with her child. The overmantel section shows Queen Victoria presenting the young Prince of Wales in an elegant ballroom setting.

WALL PAINTING
Anonymous
c. 1848
Granville Ferry, Nova Scotia
215 × 455 cm
Courtesy National Gallery of Canada

The east wall of the Croscup house reflects an attrac-
tive, if fanciful, vision of old-world civilization at the
height of the Victorian era. Scenes reminiscent of
England were especially popular in Canada in the
nineteenth century.

PORTRAIT OF WILLIAM III
Anonymous
19th century
Dufferin County, Ontario
86 × 139 cm

Found in an Orangeman's Hall near Orangeville, Ontario, this unusual oil painting of King William III appears to have been adapted from a Currier and Ives print of the same subject. It originally served as a table-top, and may have been used for ceremonial purposes in the local chapter.

Gib Jesu daß Herz In freude u. schmerz. Im leben u. tod. dif eine ist noth

Dieses schöne
Bild = Gehöret
Magdalena
Meyerin 1804

◁ PICTURE FOR MAGDALENA MEYER
Anonymous
1804
Lincoln County, Ontario
16.5 × 9.5 cm
Courtesy Jordan Museum of the Twenty

ILLUMINATED SONGBOOK
Anonymous
1804
Lincoln County, Ontario
9 × 16.5 cm
Courtesy Jordan Museum of the Twenty

The Pennsylvania-German tradition of manuscript illumination known as *Fraktur* was brought to Upper Canada around the turn of the nineteenth century. Combining decorative calligraphy with painted embellishment, most *Fraktur* compositions feature symmetrical arrangements of traditional folk motifs such as birds, hearts, and flowers. This picture for Magdalena Meyer (the '-in' is a diminutive ending indicating a little girl) is rare in Mennonite art in that it shows a human figure.

From the Mennonite settlement of Vineland in Lincoln County have survived several songbooks decorated by teachers and presented to pupils at the end of the school year. (The *Schulmeister* in a Pennsylvania-German community was customarily an expert calligrapher). Inscribed for Magdalena Meyer, 'singing student in the Clinton School', this booklet is the earliest known example of Ontario *Fraktur* containing both date and placemark.

BIRDS AND FLOWERS
Anna Weber (1814–88)
1886
Waterloo County, Ontario
16 × 10 cm

Even the folk art of strongly defined ethnic communities is not impervious to change: in the case of *Fraktur,* the pictorial element gradually became more important than the text. An example is the work of Anna Weber, a Mennonite woman who in later years turned her energies to making watercolours for friends. Most are symmetrical compositions featuring stylized bird and flower motifs without the traditional text association, although she usually did include her name and the date of completion.

PAPER CUT-OUT
Abraham Meyer
1824
Lincoln County, Ontario
39 × 32 cm

The Pennsylvania-German tradition of decorative paper-cutting
came to Upper Canada in the late nineteenth century, when the
first Mennonite settlers crossed over the Niagara River. In its sim-
plest form a symmetrical design was created by folding the paper
once before cutting. Here Abraham Meyer folded the sheet twice,
producing both horizontal and vertical symmetry.

ANGEL
Joseph D. Bauman (1815–99)
1848
Waterloo County, Ontario
9.5 × 15 cm

Joseph D. Bauman, a farmer and amateur artist, was more versatile in his *Fraktur* work than was his contemporary Anna Weber. Producing not only watercolours but bible registers for family and friends, he often based his designs on birth and baptismal certificates printed in Pennsylvania. This delightful cross-legged angel was painted for his first child, Maria, born in 1839.

LEOPARD
Anonymous
19th century
Waterloo County, Ontario
14 × 18 cm
Courtesy Conrad Grebel College Archives

This primitive watercolour proves that folk artists
were not confined to homely, everyday subjects.
With its faulty perspective, unbalanced design, and
lack of any plausible proportion, it is a classic example of naïve art. The composition seems to have
been inspired by earlier examples from southeastern
Pennsylvania.

ILLUMINATED BOOKPLATE AND GENEOLOGY
Abraham Latschaw (1799–1870)
1823
Waterloo County, Ontario
Each 34 × 21 cm
Courtesy Kitchener Public Library and
Waterloo Historical Society

A cabinet-maker and *Fraktur* artist by profession,
Abraham Latschaw immigrated from Pennsylvania
in 1822. This elaborate two-page illumination from
the bible of Benjamin Eby (1785–1853), prominent
bishop and spiritual leader of the Mennonites in
Upper Canada, comprises on the left a bookplate
and on the right a geneology of the Eby family. Early
Fraktur works such as this generally show a close
integration of text and decoration.

ROXBURGH PLACE
J. Winterborn
1868
Oxford County, Ontario
58 × 89 cm

This large watercolour is fascinating in its numerous carefully rendered details: the peacock on the right, the group on the veranda, the woman in the doorway, the stump-clearing in the field. Each of these elements is treated in isolation, however, and the resulting lack of unity marks the composition as the work of a naïve artist. Winterborn was apparently a schoolteacher in Blenheim Township.

FLOCK OF IMPORTED COTSWOLD SHEEP
Joseph Swift
1887
Toronto, Ontario
44 × 84 cm
Courtesy Royal Ontario Museum, Canadiana Gallery

PERTY. OF. LAIDLAW & JACKSON. WILTON. GROVE ONT
st Prize — Aged Ewes first Prize — Shearling Ewes first Prize — Lambs first Prize
against all classes of long wool Sheep

The enterprising artist Joseph Swift was likely hired to depict these prize-winning sheep at the annual Toronto exhibition, where proud owners would often commission paintings as records for posterity. His handling of the subject is in the best tradition of primitive art: note the contradictory shadows at the animals' feet and the trees in the centre background, enlarged to accommodate the impressive bulk of the ram.

CLIPPER SHIP MIMA MARIA
Captain Alexander McNeilledge (1791–1874)
1857
Port Dover, Ontario
15 × 20 cm
Courtesy Eva Brook Donley Museum

Alexander McNeilledge, a retired sea-captain, liked to entertain
his friends with humorous stories and sketches; his diary gives a
lively account of how he gave up seafaring to settle in the tiny
village of Port Dover, on the north shore of Lake Erie. This drawing for Joseph and Mary Culver is typical of the affectionate trib-
utes he paid to neighbouring families, in which he would christen
the ship after the wife, list the husband as master, and name
smaller boats for the children. The voyages recorded in the captions
are always fictional, and sometimes fantastic.

SONGBOOK ILLUMINATION
Francis Hughes
1813
Norfolk County, Ontario
11 × 18 cm
Courtesy Eva Brook Donley Museum

Made for Judith Humphreys (born in 1783), this songbook is an illuminated manuscript in the British tradition, as opposed to the Pennsylvania-German — the Humphreys family came from County Tyrone in Ireland. Pages inscribed with hymns and verses are interspersed with drawings of such diverse subjects as houses, peacocks, and a horse and rider, as well as the sun, moon, and stars.

PAPER CUT-OUT
Anonymous
Mid-19th century
Southwestern Ontario
34 × 46 cm

Found in the Niagara Peninsula, this extraordinarily
delicate paper cut-out was probably made as a love-
token. The dog chasing squirrels up the tree on the
right is a playful addition to the idyllic scene.

HOME SWEET HOME
Anonymous
Mid-20th century
Waterloo County, Ontario
28.5 × 43.5 cm

This rare picture of a Pennsylvania-German Mennonite homestead shows a farm on the Lexington-Conestogo Road, including the 'doddy house' built for the retiring parents on transfer of the property to a son. With livestock in the foreground, woodland and fields at the back, and neat rows of flowers here and there, this harmonious scene reflects the order and tidiness typical of a Mennonite farm.

2
SCULPTURE

The influence of high art on folk sculpture
is most evident in Quebec, where ecclesiastical sculptors
imported by the authorities in New France
established a craft tradition that was eventually
to inspire generations of self-taught carvers.
Although many continued to produce religious objects
(for more examples, see pages 94–8),
these folk artists were equally at home with down-to-earth themes:
familiar birds and animals seem to have been favourite subjects.

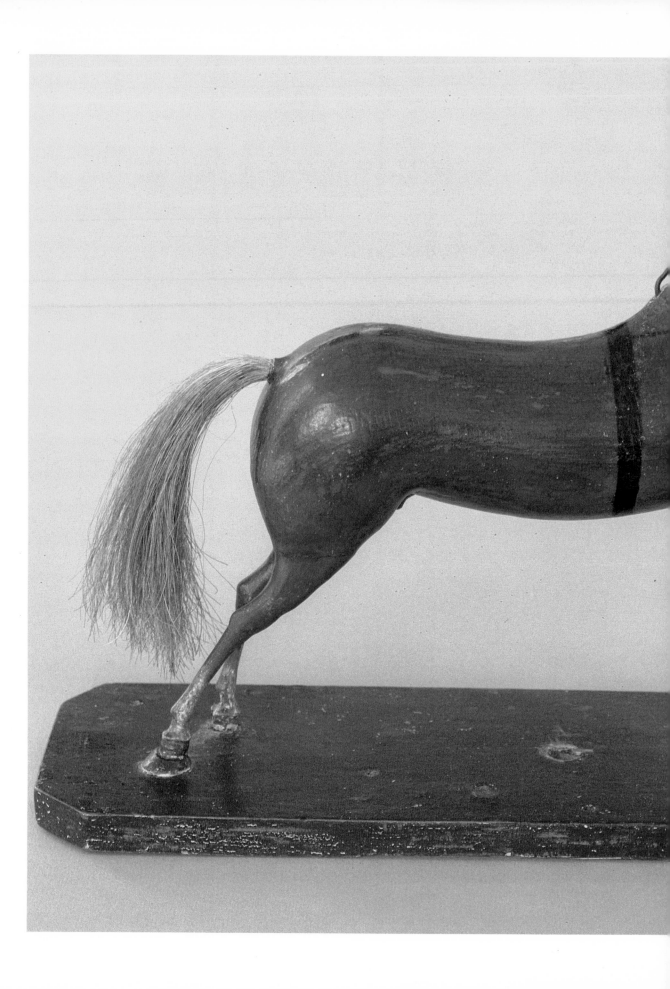

HORSE AND STANDING FIGURE
Anonymous
Late 19th century
Quebec

The tradition of wood sculpture in Quebec dates
back to the great schools of academic church
carving established in the seventeenth century;
nevertheless, the refinement of this piece is
exceptional. Perhaps one of its most striking
features is the graceful sweep of the horse's
head and neck, repeated in the curve of the tail.

◁ ARGILLITE FIGURE
Anonymous
Mid-19th century
Queen Charlotte Islands, British Columbia
37.5 × 10.5 × 14.5 cm
Courtesy British Columbia Provincial Museum

HORSE AND RIDER
Anonymous
19th century
Saint-Georges-Ouest, Quebec
32 × 25.5 cm
Courtesy National Museum of Man, Ottawa
(Canadian Centre for Folk Culture Studies)

Before 1820, most of the Haida's carvings in argillite (a carbonaceous shale) took the form of the traditional panel pipe, but European demand brought a dramatic shift in their work; by the mid-nineteenth century, their subjects included houses, ships, and public figures. This piece is believed to represent Sir James Douglas, who was appointed Governor of Vancouver Island in 1851.

According to the church files in which this robust carving was recorded, the rider represents Benedict Arnold, a figure of wavering sympathies and reputation in both Canada and the United States.

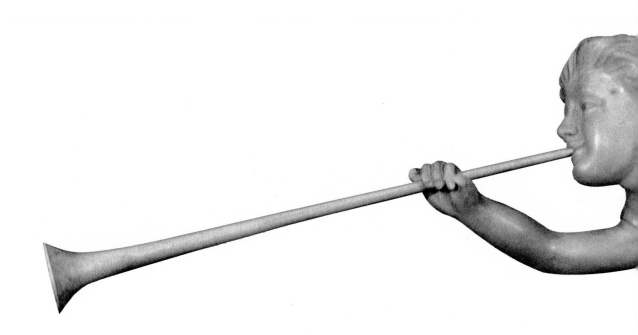

TRUMPETING ANGEL
Anonymous
Late 19th century
Quebec
41 × 155 cm
Courtesy National Museum of Man, Ottawa
(Canadian Centre for Folk Culture Studies)

The late nineteenth century witnessed a revival of large-scale sculpture recalling the figureheads carved for sailing vessels in earlier times. Now craftsmen began producing large figures for such disparate contexts as circus carousels and funeral carriages. This angel blowing a coach-horn was originally one of a pair mounted on a horse-drawn hearse.

WROUGHT-IRON ANGEL
André Parrot
19th century
Quebec
25 × 17.5 cm

André Parrot's wrought-iron angel testifies that early
Quebec craftsmen were no less adept in metal than
in wood. The hands, feet, and hair all reflect meticulous attention to detail, as does the intricately fash-
ioned belt, twisted to resemble strands of rope. The
graceful curve of the wings is repeated in the bend of
the

ROOSTER
Jean-Baptiste Côté (1832–1907)
Late 19th century
Quebec City
15 × 20 cm

Brilliance of colour and boldness of form character-
ize the work of Jean-Baptiste Côté, one of Quebec's
greatest nineteenth-century wood-carvers. Known
principally for his ships' figureheads and religious
pieces, he brought consummate skill even to simple
subjects such as this proudly strutting rooster.

WEATHERCOCK
Anonymous
Early 19th century
Quebec
Courtesy Collections d'Ethnographie du Québec

In Canada, the rooster or weathercock has become
almost synonymous with the folk art of Quebec. The
symbol apparently entered Christian iconography in
the early medieval period, after a papal edict de-
creed that it should be installed atop every church to
remind the faithful of how Peter betrayed Christ three
times before the cock crowed.

WEATHERCOCK
Anonymous
Early 19th century
Quebec
Courtesy Collections d'Ethnographie du Québec

Folk-art variations on the rooster theme are virtually
endless. In contrast to the preceding example, this
metal weathercock achieves both animation and unity of design through the imaginative use of bold
cyma curves and arabesques.

WEATHERVANE
Anonymous
19th century
Irena, Ontario
120 × 80 cm
Courtesy National Museum of Man, Ottawa
(Canadian Centre for Folk Culture Studies)

The idea of the weathervane dates back to at least
the first century B.C., when Andronicus had a bronze
Triton built for the Tower of the Winds in Athens.
Hand-cut from sheet-iron, this horse seems almost
ready to tear free from its moorings.

38

WEATHERVANE
Anonymous
Mid-19th century
Quebec
38 × 49 cm
Courtesy Royal Ontario Museum, Canadiana Gallery

Mythological subjects such as mermaids, centaurs,
and sea-serpents were introduced into weathervane
design during the nineteenth century, and many were
later mass-produced from moulds by manufacturers.
This sheet-iron dragon is a fine example of the
imaginative forms created by individual craftsmen.

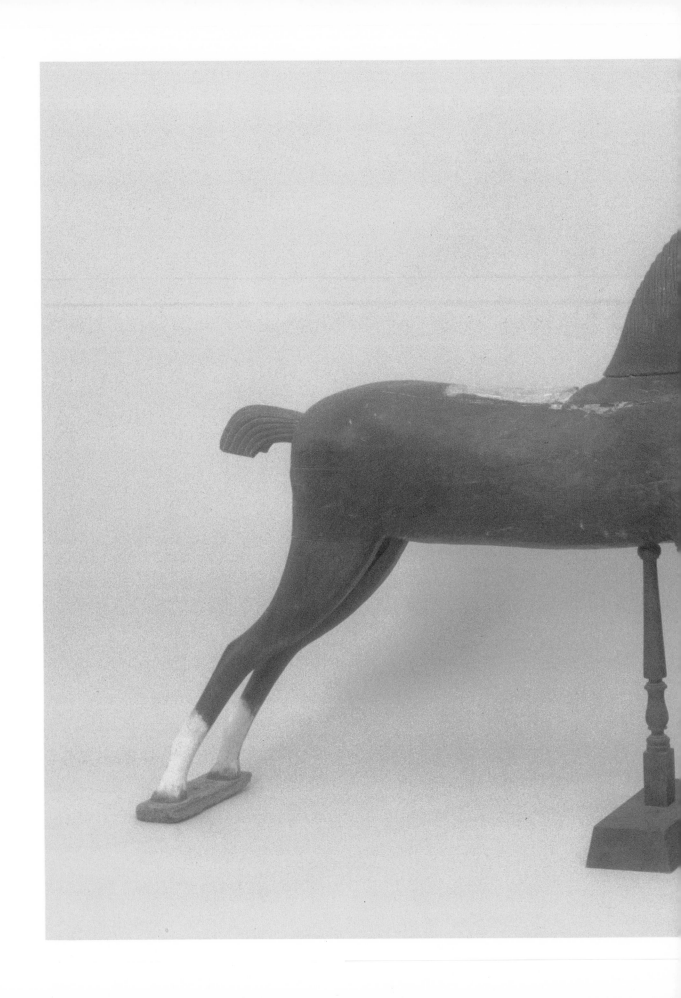

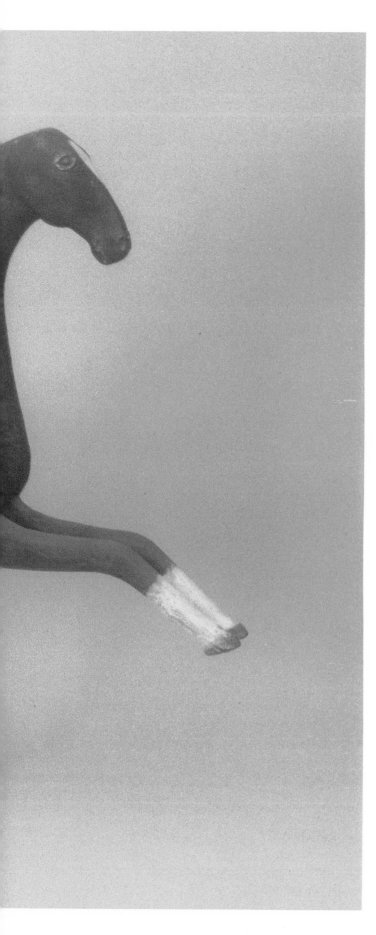

CAROUSEL HORSE
John Gemeinhardt (1826–1912)
Late 19th century
Bayfield, Ontario
115 × 153 × 23 cm

Best known as a cabinet-maker, the Huron
County craftsman John Gemeinhardt was com-
missioned by a client in Grand Bend to fashion
a carousel, from which only this horse has survived. The deeply carved features and clean
severity of line make it a sculpture of considerable power.

OWL
Damase Richard
Mid-20th century
Quebec
27.5 × 11 cm

In Quebec the name 'Richard' is almost synonymous
with wood-carving: four generations of the family
have been experts in the craft. Remarkably lifelike in
its posture, this wide-eyed owl is convincing evidence
of Damase Richard's skill.

3
TOYS
&
GAMES

Until the late nineteenth century,
all the toys and games most children ever saw
were made either in the home or by local craftsmen.
Even the mass-produced offerings of mail-order companies such as
Eaton's and Simpson's did not take the place of
hand-crafted toys for quite a long time.
In fact, some of the most appealing early twentieth-century playthings
are home-made versions of the commercial
products advertised in the catalogues,
to which the makers added their own imaginative touches.

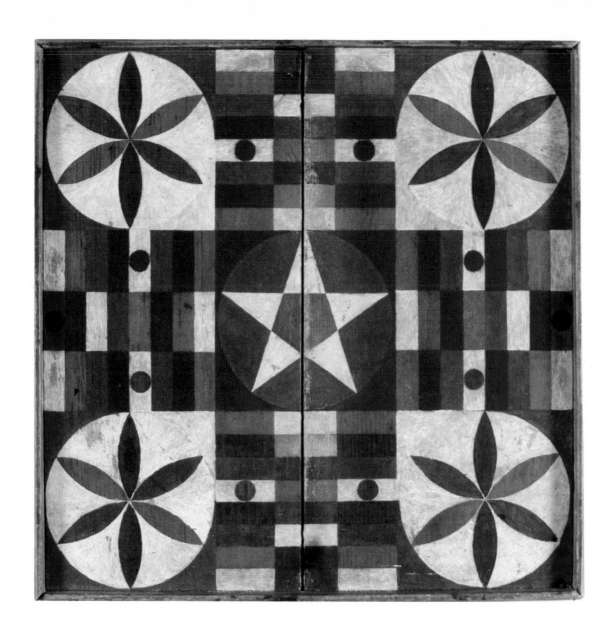

PARCHEESI BOARD
Anonymous
19th century
Lunenburg, Nova Scotia
47 × 47 cm

Among the many home-made objects that lend themselves to decoration are the wooden boards used in
popular games such as chequers and Parcheesi. The
arrangement of squares and spaces in the latter is
especially well suited to geometric treatment. Some
of the finest examples in Canada have come from the
Germanic settlements of Lunenburg County.

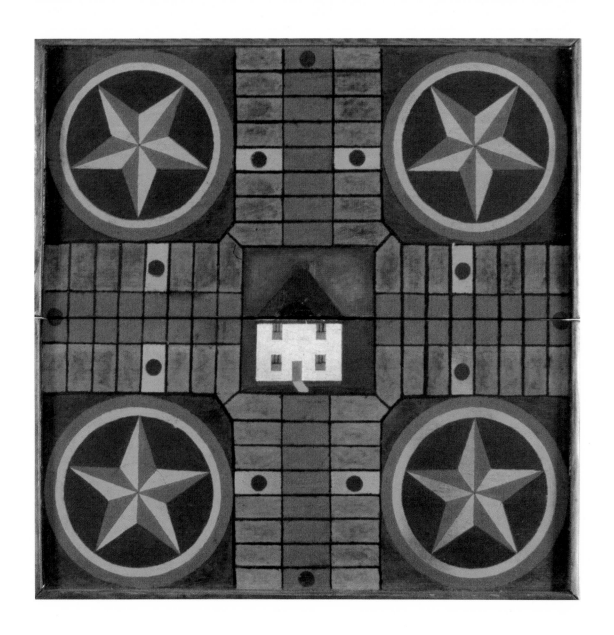

PARCHEESI BOARD
Anonymous
c. 1925
Lunenburg, Nova Scotia
56 × 55.5 cm

With a primitive-looking house marking the 'home'
section, this Parcheesi board was made by a member
of the Mason family in the town of Lunenburg. The
boldly painted circles and faceted stars are typical of
decorated furniture and household items from the
south shore of Nova Scotia.

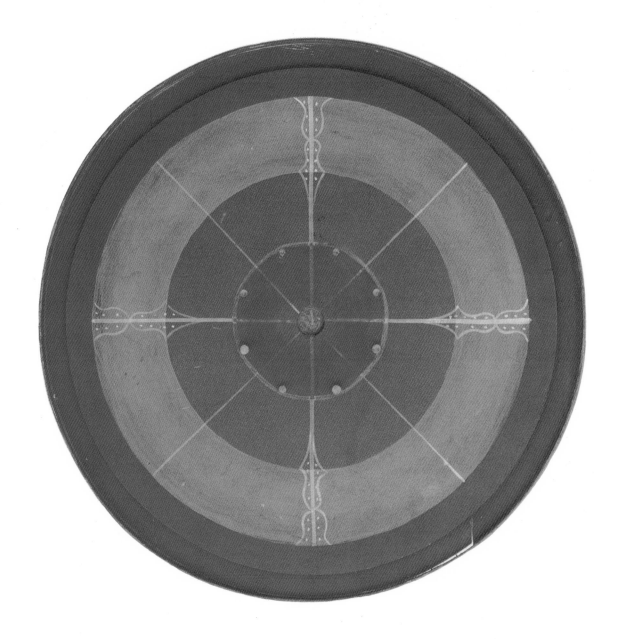

◁ CHEQUERBOARD
Anonymous
Late 19th century
Beauce County, Quebec
68.5 × 45 cm

CROKINOLE BOARD
Eckhardt Wettlaufer (1845–1919)
1875
Sebastopol, Ontario
66 cm diam.

This chequerboard includes additional decorations on either side of the playing surface. In each tray is a scene (possibly adapted from a children's story-book) painted on cardboard and mounted on the surface. A larger similar scene is painted directly on the wood of the reverse side.

The Perth County painter and wagon-maker Eckhardt Wettlaufer made this crokinole board for the fifth birthday of his son Adam, born in 1870. According to the family, the board was used for playing only on special occasions such as birthdays, and normally hung on a peg in a bedroom.

BIRD GAME
Anonymous
Late 19th century
Berlin (Kitchener), Ontario
26 × 36.5 × 36.5 cm
Courtesy Doon Pioneer Village

This game, which appears to be based on the luck of the spin, may have been made by Moritz Lindner (1816–98), a craftsman originally from Germany who advertised toys, display horses, and Christmas figures in the Kitchener area in the late nineteenth century. The stencilling on this piece resembles known examples of Lindner's work.

CHEQUERBOARD ▷
Anonymous
Late 19th century
Norfolk County, Ontario
55 × 38 cm

Maritime scenes displayed in roccoco-inspired cartouches make this chequerboard an outstanding example of late-nineteenth-century decorative art. The lighthouse and shoreline are likely those at Port Dover, where the board was found.

CARVED BIRD IN WIRE CAGE
Anonymous
c. 1920
Quebec
14 × 5 cm

A touching story is associated with this toy. Made for
a child born with Down's syndrome by her mother, it
remained a source of simple pleasure for the rest of
her life. The tiny painted bird is scarcely three centi-
metres long.

4

TEXTILES

In an age of mass-production and paint-by-number crafts,
we tend to idealize the past as a time of unbounded individual creativity.
In fairness we ought to remember that textile arts
such as weaving and embroidery
have always depended on existing patterns and available materials,
however imaginatively they may have been used.
The tradition of creative adaptation continues today,
when the floral designs for hooked rugs
are often based on commercial greeting cards,
and even a Hutterite show towel may be made with liquid embroidery.

EMBROIDERED BEDCOVER
Elsie McCullock
c. 1870
Grand Valley, Ontario
200 × 180 cm

From Dufferin County in southwestern Ontario, this elaborately embroidered bedcover might be considered in the category of 'revival' art. The idea of the basket-and-flower design on a black background was apparently inspired by eighteenth-century examples from New England.

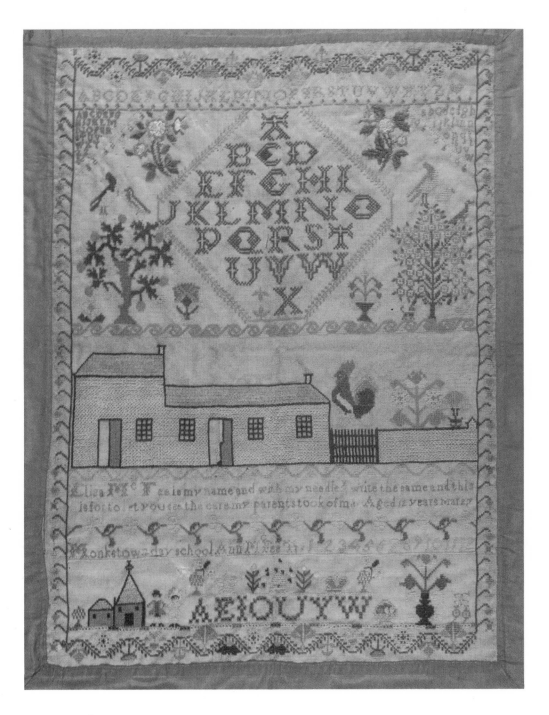

EMBROIDERED SAMPLER
Eliza McFee
19th century
Newfoundland
41 × 31 cm

Formality and realism combine in this delightful
sampler by the twelve-year-old Eliza McFee. The
difference between the two is most striking in the
juxtaposition of a highly stylized tree motif with a
realistic-looking gate and wall.

BOUTONNÉ COVERLET
Angèle Perron
c. 1885
Les Éboulements-en-Haut, Quebec
194 × 186 cm
Courtesy National Gallery of Canada

Angèle Perron's cotton-and-wool coverlet is a colourful example
of the *boutonné* decoration for which Charlevoix County is well
known. Worked in knots of wool, the patterns often take geometric forms. The two figures in the centre of this piece suggest
that it may have been made for a wedding.

EMBROIDERED SAMPLER
Agnes Wallace
1848
Eastern Ontario
29.5 × 40.5 cm

Only eight years old when she made this sampler, Agnes Wallace
depicted a menagerie ranging from the familiar dog to the 'gerif'.
Traces of pencil markings show that she drew the composition on
the cloth before embroidering it.

55

◁ QUILT
Lidia Petch Park
Mid-19th century
Gunn's Hill, Ontario
197 × 167 cm

This quilt presents an imaginative view of pioneer life, combining an Indian deer-hunt with Ontario Gothic houses of a somewhat later period. Meticulous quilting and embroidery complement the appliquéd scenes and floral border.

EMBROIDERED SHOW TOWEL
Mary Snyder
1852
Waterloo County, Ontario
130 × 50 cm

Usually made by an unmarried daughter and displayed in the family parlour, the embroidered show towel is a unique feature of the Pennsylvania-German tradition. Of special interest in this piece, worked in chain-stitch, is the horse-and-rider motif at the bottom. Conventionally the riders are shown holding swords in their upraised hands, but here the weapons have been eliminated — perhaps to remove a military connotation that would conflict with the pacifist principles of the Mennonite community.

57

HOOKED RUG
Rebecca Schweitzer
1886
New Hamburg, Ontario
119 × 90 cm

By the late nineteenth century, the relatively new technique of rug-hooking had become so popular that commercial 'catalogue' patterns were widely available. Nevertheless, there was always room for an individual like Rebecca
Schweitzer to use her own ingenuity.

HOOKED RUG
Catherine Scomoroco
Early 20th century
Kitchener, Ontario
77 × 85 cm

Simple delight in applied imagination seems the likeliest
explanation for this unique design. If a *Fraktur* illumination such as the bookplate in the Benjamin Eby bible
(p. 18) represents ethnic-traditional folk art at its best,
Catherine Scomoroco's hooked rug is a superlative expression of the individual-imaginative spirit.

PILE-WEAVE CARPET
Anastasia Lords
1923
Brilliant, British Columbia
244 × 244 cm
Courtesy Glenbow Museum

Carpets woven by the Doukhobors after their arrival in western
Canada in 1899 show the influence of an earlier period of exile in
the Russian Caucasus. A stunning example is this pile-weave rug,
in which traditional Asian motifs such as camels and peacocks
mingle with recognizably Canadian elk.

5

FURNITURE

The pieces in this section were chosen
less for their significance as particular furniture forms
than for their folk-art detail.
Most decorated furniture is immediately recognizable
as the product of a well-defined ethnic tradition.
Unfortunately, this kind of embellishment
is usually one of the first ethnic elements to disappear
as a transplanted culture is assimilated.

CHEST OF DRAWERS
Anonymous
19th century
Nova Scotia
103 × 106 × 48 cm

The difference between formal and provincial is sometimes no deeper than one or two layers of paint. If this chest were made of unadorned birch, mahogany, or cherry, it would no doubt fall into the first category, but its lively sponge-painted decoration places it firmly in the second.

CHEST OF DRAWERS
Anonymous
19th century
Quebec
90 × 87 × 42 cm

If the preceding piece can be characterized as infor-
mal, this chest of drawers is unabashedly flamboyant.
The top is covered with sunburst motifs, while the
front and sides are a garden of abstract floral designs.

FOOTSTOOL
Anonymous
19th century
New Brunswick
22 × 42 × 19 cm

This pine footstool is thought to have come from the
Saint John River Valley. Its handsome decoration
features several traditional German folk designs,
including the heart, the six-pointed compass-star,
and the whirling-sun motif.

STORAGE CHEST
Anonymous
19th century
New Brunswick
27 × 69 × 37 cm

Elaborately decorated with chip-carving in what is
often called the 'Friesian style', this storage chest is
remarkable for its strong colour and wealth of detail;
chip-carving is much more common on smaller objects such as the oval box on page 113. The chest was
reputedly made in the Saint John River area.

BUFFET
Anonymous
19th century
Quebec
124 × 87.5 × 46 cm
Courtesy National Museum of Man, Ottawa
(Canadian Centre for Folk Culture Studies)

The form of this pine buffet reflects the influence of
the American Empire style that dominated furniture
design in the second half of the nineteenth century.
Its surface decoration, however, owes little to the
style books; the fretwork and the relief carving of two
dogs on the doors are particularly unusual.

DESK
Anonymous
19th century
Iroquois, Ontario
99 × 60 × 56 cm
Courtesy Upper Canada Village

From eastern Ontario, this desk is a beautiful example of the English tradition in furniture decoration.
The large basket of flowers on the lid is reminiscent
of theorem paintings, while the grapes and floral
patterns on the front and sides recall quilt-border
designs.

LADY'S TABLE
Anonymous
19th century
Erbsville, Ontario
74 × 41 × 42 cm

This cherry-inlaid lady's table was probably used
for embroidery or other needlework. Handed down
through several generations of a family in Waterloo
County, it is said to have been made by a cabinet-
maker from Germany, who gave it to his daughter as
a wedding present.

STORAGE CHEST
Anonymous
Late 19th century
Wilno, Ontario
69 × 110 × 53 cm

A vivid example of cultural continuity is the Polish
settlement established in Ontario's Renfrew County
in the third quarter of the nineteenth century. Decorated with floral motifs typical of the Kazuby region
in northern Poland, this storage chest illustrates the
community's perpetuation of its folk-art traditions.

ARMCHAIR
Anonymous
Early 19th century
Quebec
102 × 62 × 46 cm
Courtesy Collections d'Ethnographie du Québec

Although the form of this finely proportioned armchair was common throughout eastern Canada and New England, the fretwork detail on the horizontal slats is distinctively regional. The *coeur saignant,* or bleeding heart, is a familiar feature in French Canadian folk art.

LAMP TABLE
Anonymous
19th century
Lunenburg County, Nova Scotia
73 × 49 cm
Courtesy National Museum of Man, Ottawa
(Canadian Centre for Folk Culture Studies)

A popular motif in Lunenburg County, the faceted star was used
to decorate a wide variety of objects. Here it transforms an other-
wise ordinary lamp table into a striking piece of design.

ARMOIRE
Anonymous
Late 18th century
Châteauguay, Quebec
213 × 144 × 48 cm
Courtesy Canadair Ltd.

With exuberant floral motifs filling every panel and stile, scarcely an inch of this armoire, or wardrobe, has been left unadorned. The folk-art embellishment almost obscures the formalism of the Louis XV style on which it is based.

MEDICINE CHEST
Anonymous
c. 1925
Saint-Ferdinand-de-Halifax, Quebec
100 × 43.5 × 23.5 cm
Courtesy National Museum of Man, Ottawa
(Canadian Centre for Folk Culture Studies)

The decorated medicine chest, or *pharmacie*, is a form virtually
unknown in Canada outside of Quebec. Here a spreading tree
dominates the carved and painted embellishment, which includes
paired apples, birds, and fleurs-de-lis, as well as diamonds and
other geometric designs.

WOODEN CRADLE
Anonymous
19th century
Caughnawaga, Quebec
66 × 88 × 43 cm
Courtesy Château de Ramezay

This cradle is one of a type common throughout
Quebec in the nineteenth century, but the painted
floral decoration is an unusual variation. Possibly
adapted from a wallpaper design or some other
printed source, it may have been added as an after-
thought. The childlike simplicity of the motif is well
suited to the context.

QUILLWORK CRADLE
Christianne Morris and Alexander Strum
c. 1868
Nova Scotia
73 × 98 × 52 cm
Courtesy DesBrisay Museum

Christianne Morris was a Micmac woman from Choco-
late Lake, near Halifax. The birchbark panels on
which she worked these extraordinary porcupine-quill
motifs are mounted on a pine frame reputedly made
by Alexander Strum of Mahone Bay. The cradle is
supposed to be an exact copy of one she made for
the infant Edward VII about 1841.

BUFFET
Anonymous
Early 20th century
Castlegar, British Columbia
70 × 69 × 60 cm
Courtesy Kootenay Doukhobor Historical Society

The Doukhobor settlers who left Saskatchewan in
1912 for the Kootenay region of British Columbia continued to produce boldly carved and painted furniture. The complex composition repeated on the two
doors of this buffet incorporates hearts and compass-
stars as well as the lily motif characteristic of Doukhobor design.

6

ARCHITECTURE

In architecture as in furniture,
the folk element generally falls into the ethnosyncratic category,
and is more evident in decorative features
than in overall design.
With one unusual exception,
the examples in this section are therefore
details of larger architectural structures.

CARVED BARGEBOARD
Anonymous
Mid-19th century
Lanark County, Ontario

The carved bargeboard made its first appearance as part of the Gothic revival that dominated styles in many fields in the 1830s and '40s; gradually, however, imitation of medieval designs gave way to free-spirited invention. The profusion of thistles, hearts, and fleurs-de-lis on the Allen house, on the Scotch Line just west of Perth, is one of the most sumptuous examples in Canada.

WINDOW
Anonymous
19th century
Phillipsburg, Ontario

An interesting variation on the Ontario Gothic theme is this window from a farmhouse north of Phillipsburg in Waterloo County. In general, the Germanic influence was waning by the time the Gothic style became popular, but here one can see the transition in progress. The hand-carved Germanic heart suggests a reluctant surrender of the old to the new.

MINIATURE CHURCH AND PRESBYTERY
Emile Lessard (b. 1909)
Mid-20th century
Maskinongé, Quebec

Emile Lessard based these models on photographs of Maskinongé's original church and
presbytery, built in 1783 and 1811 respectively.
Made of small stones and mortar on a scale of
one to twelve, each is fitted with hand-carved
and painted furnishings appropriate to its period.

METAL-WORK
John Mahonin
1917–18
Veregin, Saskatchewan

This finely detailed metal-work was designed for the forty arcades
that make up the verandah of the Doukhobor community home in
Veregin. Recalling the traditional decoration of Doukhobor
furniture and accessories, its beautiful floral motifs were repeated
as recently as 1959 on the gates of the town cemetery.

7

GRAVE MARKERS

One source of folk art that is frequently overlooked
is the cemetery.
Scattered among the rows of commercially produced monuments
there are almost always a few hand-crafted markers
that may point to long-forgotten episodes
in local history.
In one small southwestern Ontario burial ground, for instance,
many of the markers indicated
that the deceased had died in August 1834.
Further inquiries revealed that shortly before that time
a travelling circus had visited the area,
apparently bringing with it that dreaded disease, cholera.
The epidemic that followed
filled several small cemeteries in Waterloo County with its victims.

GRAVESTONE
Anonymous
1791
Saint John, New Brunswick

Many gravestones in eastern Canada bear a strong
resemblance to earlier examples from the United
States, suggesting that they may have been made by
United Empire Loyalists settling in the area after the
American War of Independence. The style of the
carving on this stone is nearly identical to that on
several markers in the burial grounds of St Paul's
Chapel and the Trinity Churchyard in New York City.

GRAVESTONE
Anonymous
c. 1780
Halifax, Nova Scotia

The angel-motif common to so many gravemarkers can be traced back to the pre-Christian tombs of Rome, on which winged-victory figures were often depicted bearing the soul of the deceased over the threshold to the afterlife. This example comes from Old St Paul's Burial Ground in Halifax; similar features — including the curiously twisted mouth — appear on a number of headstones in the Boston area.

GRAVESTONE
Anonymous
1796
Prescott, Ontario

In the burial ground of the 'Blue Church' overlooking the St Lawrence at Prescott are several graves of Loyalist settlers from New England. The unusually fine floral decoration and winged figure on this marker are reminiscent of examples found in the Connecticut River Valley.

WOODEN GRAVEMARKER
Anonymous
1947
Île d'Orléans, Quebec

Most of the early wooden gravemarkers in Quebec
have been replaced by modern granite headstones,
but tradition still lingers here and there. This wooden
cross in the cemetery of Saint Jean, on the south side
of the Île d'Orléans, combines religious and cultural
motifs in its merging of the cross and fleur-de-lis.

IRON GRAVEMARKER
Anonymous
1895
Maryhill, Ontario

A folk-art form little known in English communities is the cast- or
wrought-iron cross commonly found in French- or German-Catholic
cemeteries. Both kinds of iron-work are represented in this ornate
marker in the cemetery of St Boniface Church in Maryhill (originally known as Rottenburg, and later as New Germany).

8
RELIGIOUS OBJECTS

Usually modelling their work
on the sophisticated products of professional ecclesiastical artists,
self-taught craftsmen provided the furnishings
for many small local churches.
Others were inspired to bring religious art
out of the church and into their everyday lives.
While the link between art and religion
is certainly not confined to the Catholic church,
the role of the latter
has been especially important in the folk art of Quebec.

EX VOTO.
J.BT. Aucler, Louis
Bouvier, Marthe.
Féuilleteau, tous 3
Sauvés, M:chamar.

VOTIVE PAINTING
Anonymous
c. 1754
Sainte-Anne-de-Beaupré, Quebec
31 × 51.5 cm
Courtesy The Redemptorist Fathers

Traditionally, a person who had successfully
petitioned a saint for deliverance would commission an *ex-voto* as a thanksgiving offering.
This piece recounts the story of three girls who
were rescued by the miraculous intervention
of Saint Anne when their boat capsized on the
St Lawrence, between Lévis and Beaupré. The
votive painting may be the earliest form of pictorial folk art in Canada.

Marg^{te}. champagne
agé de 20. ans, un jour tout
deux noyez, Le 17. juin
1754. a 2 heures du matin,
tous 5 dans ce triste état
Se recomandant à la bi-
en heureusse Ste Ane

EX · VO TO

VOTIVE PAINTING
Anonymous
1703
Sainte-Anne-de-Beaupré, Quebec
45·5 × 54·5 cm
Courtesy The Redemptorist Fathers

In contrast to the preceding *ex-voto*, depicting the drama that occasioned the miraculous rescue, this example shows the prayers of thanksgiving for assistance already rendered. It is typical of votive painting in that it represents simultaneously events in this life and in the heavenly world beyond.

◁ CRUCIFIX
Anonymous
18th century
Charlevoix County, Quebec
60 × 38 cm

Economy of style distinguishes this crucifix with its slender corpus and simply conceived details of hands, feet, and garment. As in the wooden gravemarker (p. 87), the ends of the cross are carved in the form of fleurs-de-lis.

CRUCIFIX
Anonymous
Early 20th century
Lysanko, Saskatchewan
27.5 × 6.4 cm
Courtesy National Museum of Man, Ottawa
(Canadian Centre for Folk Culture Studies)

Small crucifixes serve many liturgical purposes in the Russian Orthodox and Ukrainian Rite Catholic churches. Carved and painted by an amateur craftsman, this piece was intended for carrying in processions. The style of the Christ-figure is based on two-dimensional Byzantine icon paintings, while the floral design is drawn from more recent Russian and eastern European folk art.

WAYSIDE CALVARY
Michel Brisset
1776
Varennes, Quebec

A crucifixion scene erected in a village or at a country crossroads,
inviting reflection and prayer, the wayside Calvary is one of Quebec's
most remarkable expressions of religious folk art. This example at
Varennes, just east of Montreal, evokes a rare feeling of serenity.

WAYSIDE CRUCIFIX
Anonymous
19th century
Gaspé area, Quebec
Courtesy Musée des Beaux-Arts de Montréal

This life-sized wayside crucifix is a superb example of religious
sculpture. Although its attenuated proportions recall the early
northern Renaissance, its calm, gentle spirit is more characteristic
of southern treatments of the subject.

CRUCIFIX WITH ANGELS
Anonymous
Late 19th century
Saint-Polycarp, Quebec
Crucifix: 50 × 21 cm
Angels: each 27 × 27 cm

This finely carved grouping comes from Soulanges
County. The angels are particularly effective, their
delicate hands and wings accentuating their forward
movement and conveying a sense of lightness and
freedom.

9

HOUSEHOLD ARTICLES

Today no shopping mall is complete
without a special kitchen boutique,
and we seem to attach almost as much importance
to the design of our cooking utensils
as we do to their functional properties.
Judging by the objects in this section,
many of our ancestors
were no less particular about the aesthetic aspect of their tools.

MAPLE-SUGAR MOULD
Anonymous
19th century
Montmagny, Quebec
26 × 20 cm
Courtesy National Museum of Man, Ottawa
(Canadian Centre for Folk Culture Studies)

Hand-carved sugar-moulds such as these may be found throughout Quebec. Designs range from simple floral motifs and human figures to bibles, churches, and even trains.

◁ MAPLE-SUGAR MOULD
Anonymous
19th century
Quebec
23.5 × 13 cm

The art of maple-sugar moulding is a French-Canadian speciality. This pine mould in the form of the characteristic *coeur saignant* (see the chair on p. 70) includes a portrait of the illustrious explorer Jacques Cartier.

'ISAAC BROCK' WOOD-BLOCK
Anonymous
19th century
Quebec
17.5 × 12.5 cm
Courtesy Château de Ramezay

Wishing 'Success to Commerce and Peace to the World', this tribute to 'The Hero of Upr Canada' commemorates Sir Isaac Brock's death at the Battle of Queenston Heights in the War of 1812. The classical urn flanked by wreath-bearing angels may have been adapted from painted memorials or embroidered mourning pictures of the period.

SCRIMSHAW POWDER-HORN
George Freil
c. 1800
Lunenburg County, Nova Scotia
6 × 25 cm
Courtesy DesBrisay Museum

Scrimshaw—decorative carving in horn, ivory, shell,
or bone—was a traditional pastime of whalers and
other seamen. This richly embellished powder-horn
is typical of the scrimshaw work produced throughout the Atlantic provinces and New England.

COAT-RACK
Anonymous
1905
Veregin, Saskatchewan
16.5 × 101 cm

Inscribed with the initials 'B.I.J.', this pine coat-rack illustrates the Doukhobors' traditional taste for ornament in household objects. The strong turnings on the pegs are typical of Doukhobor furniture.

CRADLE-BOARD ▷
Anonymous
Late 19th century
Quebec
Courtesy McCord Museum

Sometimes the work of native people seems to reflect the influence of European decorative traditions: see, for example, the quillwork cradle on page 75. The carved and painted decoration of this Iroquois cradle-board recalls Pennsylvania-German folk art both in its subject matter and in its symmetrical composition.

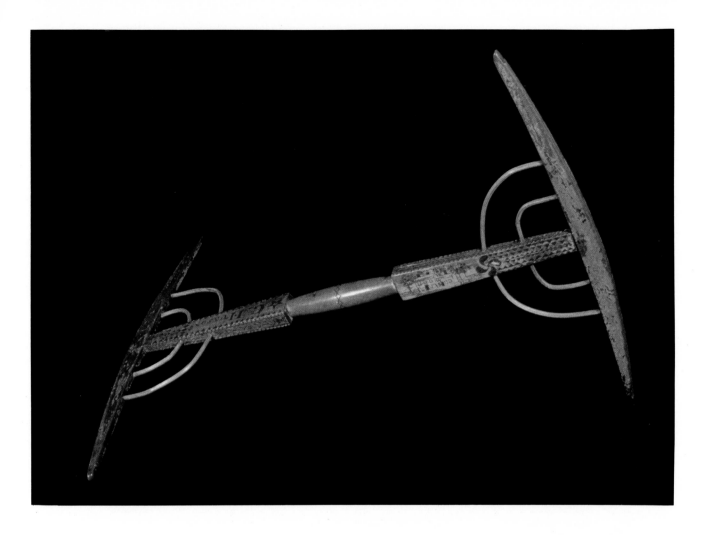

NIDDY-NODDY
Anonymous
19th century
Nova Scotia
36.5 × 49.5 cm

The tools used in domestic crafts such as spinning and weaving seem to lend themselves to personalization. Every side of this birch niddy-noddy (or yarn-winder) is lavished with decoration, including hearts, stars, vines, a whirling sun, and a house and trees, in addition to the name 'G. Hunson'.

◁ APPLE-PEELER
David Byer
1843
Markham, Ontario
49 × 19.5 × 73 cm
Courtesy Black Creek Pioneer Village

From the Mennonite settlement at Markham, this apple-peeler is another example of the decorative attention often paid to the homeliest implements. Shallow holes punched into the surface create a composition incorporating virtually every important motif from the Pennsylvania-German tradition.

STONEWARE CROCK
Franklin P. Goold and Company
c. 1859–67
Brantford, Ontario
36 × 35 cm
Courtesy Royal Ontario Museum, Canadiana Gallery

Stoneware manufacturing in Ontario began with the establish-
ment of a pottery at Brantford in 1849; this storage crock was made
during the proprietorship of Franklin P. Goold, an entrepreneur
originally from New Hampshire. The decoration was incised in
the clay before the glaze was applied.

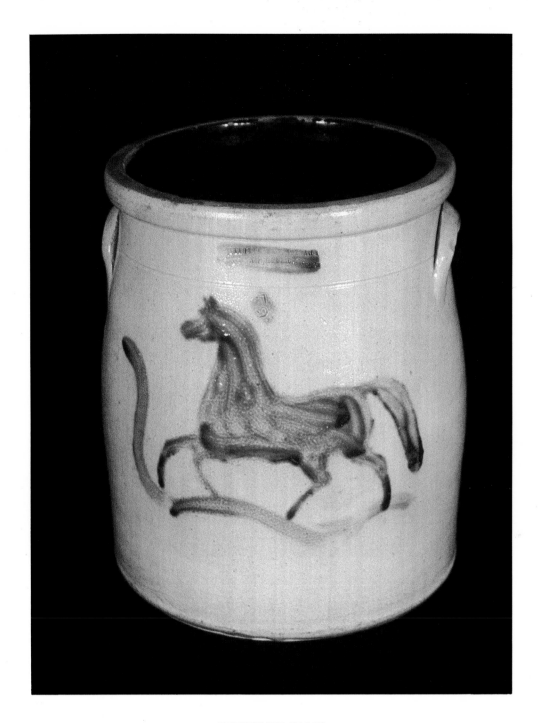

STONEWARE CROCK
David Flack and Isaac Van Arsdale
Late 19th century
Cornwall, Ontario
35.5 × 28 cm

The pottery established by David Flack and Isaac Van Arsdale in 1869 flourished for nearly forty years. The horse design on this crock is unusual in their work; most of the company's wares were decorated with a stylized bird.

EARTHENWARE SUGAR-BOWLS
Anonymous
19th century
Ontario
19 × 13.5 cm; 15 × 13 cm

These earthenware sugar-bowls were found in different places; however, the resemblance between the
dog and the lion is strong enough to suggest that they
were made by the same person, most likely a professional potter. Requiring a high degree of skill, they
may well have been intended as gifts or evidence of
his craftsmanship.

10
DECORATED BOXES

In addition to personal papers
such as wills, marriage certificates, and birth records,
most people have a few small treasures to call their own:
family heirlooms, trinkets, lucky charms.
All of these items require some place of safekeeping.
Today we may simply go to the bank and rent a safety-deposit box,
but in the past private effects were generally kept at home,
often in a hand-crafted box.
Whether intended for the maker's own use or as a gift for a loved one,
a small box provided an ideal background for fanciful decoration.

DOCUMENT BOX
Joseph Laurent
1866
Montreal area, Quebec
12.5 × 26 × 17.5 cm

In the inscription on the top of this document box
Joseph Laurent identified himself as a painter (phon-
etically spelled *pintre*) and carriage-maker. The un-
derside of the lid depicts the steamship *Beaver* (or, as
he spelled it, *Biveur*), which plied the inland water-
ways from Montreal to the Great Lakes.

OVAL BOX
Anonymous
Quebec
19th century
17 × 35.5 × 24.5 cm

Many boxes with lids carved in the Friesian style have
been found in Quebec, but few show the refinement
of detail evident in this piece. The fan-like devices at
the ends, flanking the conventional circles and arcs,
are particularly unusual.

DECORATED BOX
Anonymous
19th century
Quebec
17.5 × 30 × 21 cm

Carved in relief then painted, the decoration on this
box combines the exotic image of a lion with patri-
otic beavers on either end and a central design com-
posed of four fleurs-de-lis.

DOMED BOX
Anonymous
19th century
Quebec

One of the most fascinating qualities of folk art is its
tendency to combine quite different kinds of embellishment. In addition to a colourful graphic decoration, the maker of this box gave it a texture, cross-
hatching the surface to resemble tooled leather.

PAINTED BOX
Captain Alexander McNeilledge
1867
Port Dover, Ontario
12.7 × 28.6 × 22.2 cm

Captain Alexander McNeilledge (see p. 22) was an
enthusiastic supporter of Confederation, and to cele-
brate the great event he transformed an ordinary
candle box into this whimsical memorial. Some of
the minute inscriptions repeated along the borders
contain a brief self-portrait: 'Captain Alex. McNeilledge – 76 years – Use no specks – Chew no tobacco –
Take only a wee drop as required'. Others simply
sum up with the statement 'Not bad for an old
Scotchie'.

GLOSSARY

Adam style

A mid-eighteenth-century furniture style based on classical models and emphasizing linear or rectilinear features as opposed to the curvilinear baroque.

American Empire style

A furniture style dominated by columns, capitals, cyma curves, and other decorative features associated with ancient Greece and Rome. Related to the neo-classical style in architecture, it became popular in the mid-nineteenth century.

Chip-carving

A method of carving with a knife or chisel in which an area of the surface is chipped, then cut away; used to produce geometric motifs.

Compass-star

The design resulting when a compass is used to draw intersecting arcs radiating from a common centre.

Cyma curve

In architecture and furniture, a contour or profile consisting of a curve that is partly concave and partly convex.

Earthenware

Pottery of baked or hardened clay fired at a low temperature.

Fraktur

Decorative calligraphy in the Swiss-German tradition, brought to Pennsylvania in the eighteenth century and subsequently to Canada by the Mennonites who settled in southwestern Ontario after 1786.

Fretwork

The decorative effect achieved by cutting completely through a board or panel with a knife or small saw. Stencils were often used to trace the design onto the surface.

Friesian style

In folk art, a style of carved or painted decoration associated with Friesland in the Netherlands as well as areas of England and northwestern France. The carving is characteristically geometric, using intersecting arcs and compass-circles.

Gothic revival

In architecture and furniture, a term referring to the mid-nineteenth-century vogue for features originating in the twelfth century, including pointed arches, ribbed vaults, and decorative fretwork.

Illumination

Originally the pictorial decoration accompanying the hand-lettered text of bibles and other books; the term is frequently broadened to include the folk-art enbellishment of any text or document.

Limner

A term used in the British Isles and the northeastern United States for a nonacademic portrait artist whose primary occupation might have been coach-, sign-, or even house-painting. Before the advent of photography, most family portraits in eastern Canada and New England were painted by itinerant limners.

Louis XV style

In architecture and furniture, a style emphasizing assymetrical panelling or profiles and baroque conventions such as carved shells and scrolls.

Overmantel picture

A landscape or other scene painted directly on the wall above a fireplace mantel; popular in the eighteenth century.

Sheraton style

A furniture style based on Thomas Sheraton's *Drawing Book* of 1792–5, emphasizing fine turnings in contrast to the tapered square leg of Hepplewhite design; popular in North America in the first half of the nineteenth century.

Sponge-painting

Literally, a technique in which paint is applied with a sponge; generally the term is used to refer to any painted decoration achieved by random daubing rather than brushwork.

Stile

In case furniture, one of the supporting members framing doors or panels within doors.

Stoneware

Opaque vitrified ceramic ware, fired at a high temperature.

Theorem painting

A technique of painting on paper or silk by means of stencils, one or more for each colour; taught to the daughters of well-to-do families throughout the early nineteenth century.

SELECTED REFERENCES

GENERAL THEORETICAL WORKS

Ames, Kenneth. *Beyond Necessity: Art in the Folk Tradition.* Winterthur, Del.: The Winterthur Museum, 1977.

Carraher, Ronald G. *Artists in Spite of Art.* New York: Van Nostrand Reinhold Co., 1970.

Glassie, Henry. *Patterns in the Material Folk Culture of the Eastern United States.* Philadelphia: University of Philadelphia Press, 1968.

Kallir, Jane. *The Folk Art Tradition.* New York: Viking Press, 1981.

Schorsch, Anita, and Martin Greif. *The Morning Stars Sang: The Bible in Popular and Folk Art.* New York: Universe Books, 1978.

BACKGROUND — EUROPEAN AND AMERICAN

Andrews, Ruth, ed. *How to Know American Folk Art.* New York: E.P. Dutton, 1977.

Ayres, James. *British Folk Art.* Woodstock, N.Y.: The Overlook Press, 1977.

Cuisenier, Jean. *French Folk Art.* Tokyo: Kodansha International, 1976.

Hansen, H.J., ed. *European Folk Art in Europe and the Americas.* New York: McGraw-Hill Book Co., 1968.

Kauffman, Henry J. *Pennsylvania Dutch American Folk Art.* New York: Dover Publications, 1964.

Lipman, Jean, and Alice Winchester. *The Flowering of American Folk Art, 1776-1876.* New York: Viking Press, 1974.

Schlee, Ernst. *German Folk Art.* Tokyo: Kodansha International, 1980.

Weiser, Frederick S., and Howell J. Heaney. *The Pennsylvania German Fraktur of the Free Library of Philadelphia* (2 vols.). Breiningsville, Penn.: The Pennsylvania German Society, 1977.

CANADA — GENERAL

Abrahamson, Una. 'Treenware and Wooden Utensils'. In Donald B. Webster, ed., *The Book of Canadian Antiques.* Toronto: McGraw-Hill Ryerson Ltd, 1974.

Adamson, Anthony, and John Willard. *The Gaiety of Gables: Ontario's Architectural Folk Art.* Toronto: McClelland and Stewart Ltd, 1974.

Art Gallery of Windsor. *Celebration: The Marjorie Larmon Collection of 19th and 20th Century Folk Art in Canada.* Introduction by Jim Sherman. Windsor, Ont.: Art Gallery of Windsor, 1982.

Burnham, Harold B., and Dorothy K. Burnham. *Keep Me Warm One Night: Early Handweaving in Eastern Canada.* Toronto: University of Toronto Press, 1972.

Conroy, Mary. *300 Years of Canada's Quilts.* Toronto: Griffin House, 1976.

Dalhousie Art Gallery. *Decorated Nova Scotia Furnishings.* Foreword by Tom Lackey. Dalhousie, N.S.: Dalhousie Art Gallery, 1978.

Dobson, Henry and Barbara Dobson. *The Early Furniture of Ontario and the Atlantic Provinces.* Toronto: M.F. Feheley Publishers, 1974.

_____. *A Provincial Elegance.* Kitchener, Ont.: Electrohome Ltd, 1982.

Field, Richard. *Gamesboards.* Introduction by Elliott Avedon. Halifax: Art Gallery of Nova Scotia, 1981.

Hanks, Carole. *Early Ontario Gravestones.* Toronto: McGraw-Hill Ryerson Ltd, 1974.

Harper, J. Russell. *People's Art: Naïve Art in Canada.* Ottawa: The National Gallery of Canada, 1973-74.

_____. *A People's Art: Primitive, Naïve, Provincial and Folk Art Painting in Canada.* Toronto: University of Toronto Press, 1974.

Holmes, Janet. 'Toys and Games'. In Donald B. Webster, *The Book of Canadian Antiques.* Toronto: McGraw-Hill Ryerson Ltd, 1974.

SELECTED REFERENCES

Kobayashi, Terry. 'Local Paintings Tour Canada: Ora C. Walper and J.J. Kenyon'. *Waterloo Historical Society*, 1974.

McKendry, Ruth. *Quilts and Other Bed Coverings in the Canadian Tradition.* Toronto: Van Nostrand Reinhold Ltd, 1979.

Mattie, Joan I. *Folk Art in Canada.* Plattsburgh, N.Y.: Clinton County Historical Museum, 1981.

Mattie, Wesley C. 'Museum of Man Folk Art Collection'. *Canadian Antiques and Art Review*, November 1979.

Newlands, David L. *Early Ontario Potters: Their Craft and Trade.* Toronto: McGraw-Hill Ryerson Ltd, 1979.

Pain, Howard. *The Heritage of Upper Canadian Furniture.* Toronto: Van Nostrand Reinhold Ltd, 1978.

Price, Ralph, and Patricia Price. *'Twas Ever Thus: A Selection of Eastern Canadian Folk Art.* Toronto: M.F. Feheley Publishers, 1979.

Schackleton, Philip. *The Furniture of Old Ontario.* Toronto: Macmillan of Canada, 1973.

Symons, Scott. *Heritage: A Romantic Look at Early Canadian Furniture.* Toronto: McClelland and Stewart Ltd, 1971.

Tilney, Philip V.R. *Artifacts from the CCFCS Collections: Sampling No. 1.* Ottawa: National Museum of Man Mercury Series (no. 5), 1973.

Trask, Deborah. *Life How Short, Eternity How Long: Gravestone Carving and Carvers in Nova Scotia.* Halifax: Nova Scotia Museum, 1978.

Webster, Donald Blake. *The Book of Canadian Antiques.* Toronto: McGraw-Hill Ryerson Ltd, 1974.

Willson, Nancy. 'Decorative Ironwork'. In Donald B. Webster, *The Book of Canadian Antiques.* Toronto: McGraw-Hill Ryerson Ltd, 1974.

CANADA – ETHNIC AND REGIONAL

Barbeau, Marius. *I Have Seen Quebec.* Toronto: Macmillan of Canada, 1957.

————. *Quebec: Where Ancient France Lingers.* Toronto: Macmillan of Canada, 1936.

Bird, Michael S. *Beyond Survival: Ontario-German Decorative Arts in The Queen's Bush.* Bruce County Museum and Ontario Heritage Foundation, 1980.

————. 'Doukhobor Decorative Arts in Canada'. *Canadian Folklore*, Spring 1983.

————. *Ontario Fraktur: A Pennsylvania German Folk Tradition in Early Canada.* Toronto: M.F. Feheley Publishers, 1977.

————. 'Pennsylvania German Parallels: Decorative Arts of Lancaster County and Ontario'. *Canadian Antiques and Art Review*, October 1979.

————. 'A Spirit of Exuberance: Germanic Decorative Arts of Nova Scotia and Ontario'. *Canadian Antiques and Art Review*, September, 1979.

————, and Terry Kobayashi. *A Splendid Harvest: Germanic Folk and Decorative Arts in Canada.* Toronto: Van Nostrand Reinhold Ltd, 1981.

Boily, Lise and Jean-François Blanchette. *The Bread Ovens of Quebec.* Ottawa: National Museums of Canada, 1979.

Bouchard, Laurent. *Courtepointes Québécoises.* Quebec: Ministère des Affaires culturelles, 1977.

Carpenter, Carole Henderson. *Many Voices: A Study of Folklore Activities in Canada and Their Role in Canadian Culture.* Ottawa: National Museums of Canada, 1979.

Casanova, Jacques-Donat, and Armour Landry. *America's French Heritage.* Quebec: La Documentation Française and The Quebec Official Publishers, 1976.

Dupont, Jean-Claude. *Histoire populaire de l'Acadie.* Ottawa: Les Éditions Leméac, Inc., 1978.

Dwyer, Ruth. *Mennonite Decorative Arts.* Hamilton, Ont.: McMaster University Art Gallery, 1981.

Good, E. Reginald. *Anna's Art.* Kitchener, Ont.: private printing, 1976.

Johannesen, Stanley, and Michael S. Bird. *Furniture and Fraktur: An Exhibition of Artifacts from Waterloo County and Germanic Ontario.* Waterloo, Ont.: University of Waterloo Art Gallery, 1977.

Kobayashi, Terry. 'David B. Horst (1873-1965): St. Jacobs Woodcarver'. *Waterloo County Historical Society*, 1977.

————. 'Folk Art in Stone: Pennsylvania German Gravestones in Ontario'. *Waterloo Historical Society*, 1982.

————. 'Folk Art in Wood'. *Canadian Antiques and Art Review*, March 1980.

————. 'Fred G. Hoffman (1845-1926): Waterloo County Itinerant Woodcarver'. *Waterloo Historical Society*, 1981.

Lessard, Michael, and Huguette Marquis. *L'Art traditionnel au Québec.* Montreal: Les Éditions de l'homme, 1975.

Macnair, Peter, Alan L. Hoover, and Kevin Neary. *The Legacy: Continuing Traditions of Canadian Northwest Coast Indian Art.* Victoria: British Columbia Provincial Museum, 1980.

McMurray, A. Lynn. 'Ontario German Decorative Arts'. In Donald B. Webster, *The Book of Canadian Antiques.* Toronto: McGraw-Hill Ryerson Ltd, 1974.

Musée du Québec. *Arts populaires du Québec.* Quebec: Musée du Québec, 1975.

————. *Folk Art Treasures of Quebec,* Quebec and Toronto: Ontario-Quebec Permanent Commission, 1980.

————. *Sculpture traditionnelle du Québec.* Quebec: Musée du Québec, 1967.

Palardy, Jean. *The Early Furniture of French Canada.* Toronto: Macmillan of Canada, 1963.

Patterson, Nancy-Lou. 'Anna Weber (1814-1888): Waterloo County Fraktur Artist'. *Mennonite Life*, December 1975.

————. *Canadian Native Art.* Toronto: Collier-Macmillan Canada, 1973.

————. 'The Iron Cross and the Tree of Life'. *Ontario History*, March 1976.

————. *Mennonite Traditional Arts of the Waterloo Region and Southern Ontario.* Kitchener, Ont.: The Kitchener-Waterloo Art Gallery, 1974.

————. *Swiss-German and Dutch-German Mennonite Traditional Art in the Waterloo Region, Ontario.* Ottawa: National Museums of Canada, 1979.

————. Michael S. Bird, et al. *Primitive and Folk Art.* Waterloo, Ont.: University of Waterloo Art Gallery, 1976.

————, and Michael S. Bird. *A Germanic Flavour: Folk Art of the Waterloo Region and Other Germanic Settlements of Canada.* Kitchener, Ont.: Kitchener-Waterloo Art Gallery, 1979.

Porter, John R., and Léopold Désy. *Calvaires et croix de chemins du Québec.* Montreal: Hurtubise, 1973.

'Prairie Folk Art' (special issue). *Artscanada* 230-1 (October-November 1979).

Séguin, Robert-Lionel. *Les Moules du Québec.* Ottawa: National Museums of Canada, 1963.

Tarasoff, Koozman J. *Traditional Doukhobor Folkways.* Ottawa: National Museum of Man Mercury Series (no. 20), 1978.

Thériault, Léon. *Images de l'Acadie.* Montreal: Hurtubise, 1980.

Thomas, Jane. *Playful Objects: An Exhibition in Celebration of Fun.* Edmonton: 75th Anniversary Commission and Alberta Culture, Visual Arts, 1980.

Trudel, Jean. *La sculpture ancienne du Québec, manifestation d'art populaire.* Vie des Arts, 1973.

Webster, Donald B. 'Pennsylvania and Ontario Earthenwares: A Comparative View'. *Rotunda* 2 (Winter 1969).

Whitehead, Ruth Holmes. *Elitekey: Micmac Material Culture from 1600 A.D. to the Present.* Halifax: Nova Scotia Museum, 1980.

Woodcock, George, and Ivan Avakumovic. *The Doukhobors.* Toronto: Oxford University Press, 1968.